More Verses

Poetry & Songs Inspired by One Man's Life

Adrian Young

More Verses

Copyright © 2024 by Adrian Young

All rights reserved.

No part of this publication may be reproduced, stored in a retrieval system, or transmitted in any form or by any means, electronic, mechanical, photocopying, recording, or otherwise, without the prior permission of both the copyright owner and the publisher of the book.

Adrian Young asserts the moral right to be identified as the author of this work in accordance with the Copyright, Designs and Patents Act 1988.

All content has been created by Adrian Young, except Burning Bridges, Here I Go Again, Millionaire (Better With You), and The Last Chance Saloon, all of which were co-written with Sean Clack.

First Edition—Published in 2024.

ISBN 9798344420097 (Paperback)

Cover Design by One Legged Kiwi Illustration

Rear Cover Photography by James Norman Portrait

For Toni, Amelie, Emily, and Sophia

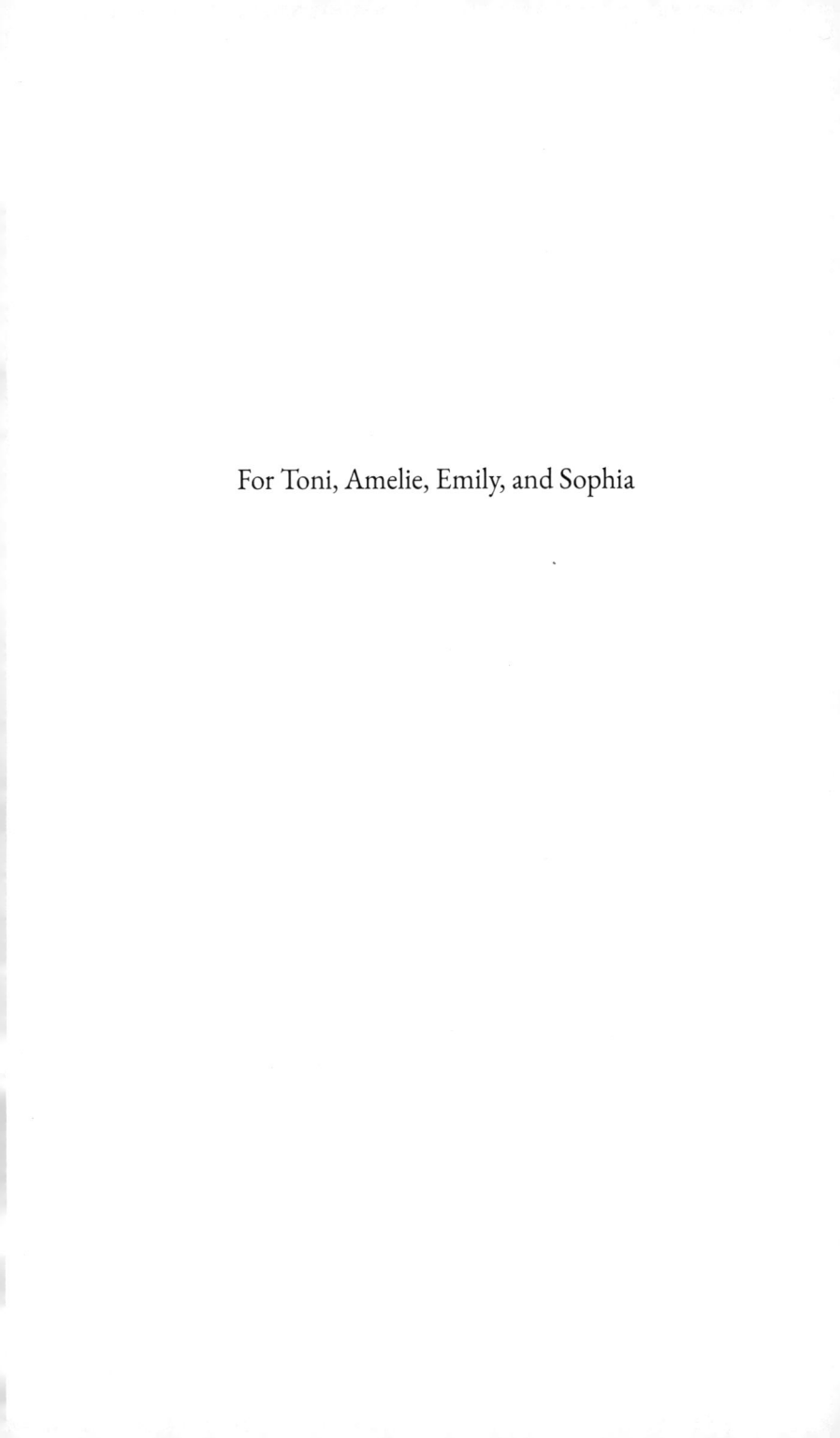

Also by Adrian Young

My Verses: An Anthology of Poems and Songs Based on One Man's Trials and Tribulations

Available at *https://amzn.to/3BtiiFb*

You can find love, you can find peace
You can find everything in between
You can find hope, you can find joy
You can find everything that you're looking for

About the Author

They say we are a product of our environment. For better or worse, I am a product of a British coastal town called Great Yarmouth.

Historically, my hometown was home to a soaring fishing trade. It was also known as one of the top seaside resorts in Britain, and welcomed many of the top pop stars of the era, including The Who and The Beatles.

Nowadays, it's best known for the chips sold on the town's ever-dwindling market, along with the high levels of deprivation within the area.

I'm not too sure what this says about me, other than I love the market chips.

Nevertheless, the town has character, and perhaps it is this, as well as the characters *within* it, that has made me into the man I have become.

Growing up, I attended two local schools; Herman and Oriel. In those days, Oriel was well-renowned for being a bit of a rough school, and had its fair share of bullying and playground fights, but I pulled through okay.

I haven't even reached 40 yet, but it's sad to see that some of my fellow students have already passed away, whilst others have suffered immeasurable pain in their lives.

Whilst I never hated school, I had little passion for it. My only enthusiasm became evident when attending English lessons, which allowed me to be creative in a manner which felt extremely fluid to me.

Whilst the rest of my school life is almost entirely forgettable, I still vividly recall my English teacher and the classroom in which those lessons took place.

After leaving school in 2001, I went straight into full-time work, as I lacked the passion for any particular field with which to attend college or university to study. Besides, like many youngsters, the lure of earning my own money was far too tempting.

It would be another two years before I really dedicated time to writing, when, in 2003, I joined my first band.

After seeing a postcard advert in the window of Allens Music Centre in Great Yarmouth, I called the listed number, and spoke to Graham Stacey.

As a local singer and songwriter, Graham was looking for a rhythm guitarist for his band, The Open Shells.

Graham undoubtedly pushed me to write my own songs. He was the first person which I knowingly met who had composed his own tracks, and I wanted to do the same.

But these things take time. As with any craft, you have to learn and develop it—this is my excuse for some utterly terrible lyrics at 18!

By this time, I was heavily submersing myself in an extremely eclectic music collection, from the timeless folk of Bob Dylan, the happy pop of the early Beatles, and the sometimes slightly offensive Eminem.

I consumed music at every opportunity available, and it quickly helped me hone my ability to write my material.

Besides music, I allowed the world around me to provide inspiration. From the venue in which my band rehearsed, to the random guy on the street, and the regular Saturday night drunken fights I witnessed in my local pubs—it all helped my creative juices flow.

One of the main turning points for me was when I introduced my song 'Hudson House' (as featured in *My Verses*) to my bandmates. Having them tell me it was 'great', and for them to spend the time helping me develop and perform the song was a memory I shall never forget.

Had they have responded by shaking their heads and forgetting about it, I may have released none of my material to the world.

In August 2018, my daughter Amelie was born. She ignited not only my passion for life, but my desire to write.

With her arrival came a flourish of inspiration and enthusiasm that had somewhat dwindled into the backdrop.

I began to perform more frequently, not only as part of various bands but also as one half of several acoustic duos, and, occasionally, I would face my fears and perform as a solo artist.

By early 2022, it became apparent that I was sitting on a substantive collection of material, so I decided to publish an anthology of my work.

In December of that year, I released my first book, *My Verses*, which I was, and am, extremely proud of.

Upon its release, the spark within me was once more ignited, and I spent every opportunity writing, performing, and brainstorming ways in which to utilise my passion for writing.

With the urge to perform thoroughly reignited, I formed a new band—The Craft—which focused on the creation and performance of original material, in tandem with covers of popular music from the 50s and 60s.

It was within The Craft that I first started collaborating with another writer, Sean Clack. Along with Nick Kitson, Hank 'Bemarvin' Shuckford, and his son, James Shuckford, I was provided a platform to develop and perform my own musical creations.

This brings us nicely to now—December 2024—preparing for the release of my second book you now hold within your hands. May many more follow.

Enjoy the book.
Adrian.

Contents

Introduction		XIX
1.	You Can Find...	1
2.	A Political Broadcast	3
3.	Never Be Alone	5
4.	Kiss On Your Forehead	8
5.	It's Getting Better	9
6.	Home Alone	12
7.	The Executioner	14
8.	Burning Bridges	16
9.	Break Down	18
10.	Blue-Eyed, Blonde-Haired Lover	20
11.	Caught in a Haze	22
12.	Acting the Fool	24
13.	What Makes a Man?	27

14.	Break Me Down/Lift Me Up	31
15.	Wherever You Go	34
16.	Flying	36
17.	Covertly Caring	38
18.	High and Mighty	40
19.	She's Left Home	41
20.	Stupid Cupid	44
21.	The Day We Left	47
22.	These Days	49
23.	Banned	51
24.	Yesterday's Another Day	52
25.	Us and the World	54
26.	Watch It All Go Wrong	56
27.	Won't Fade Away	59
28.	You Can't Fool Me	60
29.	What Is the Difference?	62
30.	Bumpy Ride	63
31.	Playing Games	65
32.	Here I Go Again	67

33.	I Don't Want War	69
34.	Senses	71
35.	Yesterday	73
36.	Sidewalk	75
37.	You Should Know	78
38.	Time Flies Away	80
39.	The Best Is Yet to Be	82
40.	Dream	83
41.	Time to Go	84
42.	Guilty Hill	85
43.	Millionaire (Better With You)	87
44.	Never Easy	90
45.	Save Me	92
46.	Fool on the Run	95
47.	The Last Chance Saloon	97
48.	What Were You Expecting?	100
49.	Exit Door	103
50.	I Feel Alive	105
51.	Final Thoughts	107

52. Thank You   109

Introduction

In December 2022, I published my first book, *My Verses: An Anthology of Poems and Songs Based Upon One Man's Trials and Tribulations*.

Born from a realisation that I was sitting on a vast collection of work that I mostly kept hidden away in notebooks or scribbled upon scraps of paper, I began sifting through all my creations.

Scattered around my house and secreted in various folders and tattered boxes, I unearthed a treasure trove of songs and poetry I had long since forgotten.

In compiling the content for *My Verses*, I chose a collection of which was important to me, and of which I hold dear.

It is a big undertaking to allow the world to read something which allows for an insight into your personal life, and it wasn't a decision I took lightly.

Several of the compositions I published enforced doubt in my mind whether I was content with allowing the reader to step inside my conscience.

We all have regrets, secrets, and skeletons within our metaphorical closets. I, too, am guilty of keeping things to myself, hoping they'll simply go away.

Something I have learnt in life is that, whilst some things are best kept secret, it can be enlightening and incredibly beneficial to face up to your demons and to express your emotions in whichever way is effective for you.

For me, writing is a productive outlet and my preferred form of expressionism.

Following the release of *My Verses*, I felt as though a weight had been lifted off of my shoulders. I had finally achieved one of my life goals—to publish a book—and it undoubtedly gave me the drive to continue to write.

This determination was further exacerbated once *My Verses* reached number one on Amazon's *Free Poetry Anthologies* chart within two days of being released. What an incredible achievement!

Within days, I began to sift through my paperwork folders, old books, and dusty USB drives, seeking any other compositions that were not included within *My Verses*.

I began reading more poetry from other authors, which allowed me to broaden my horizons and explore other avenues for inspiration.

I quickly got to work on several other projects, and within weeks, I had multiple writing projects in progress, covering various genres and styles.

As was the case with *My Verses*, this book contains a mixing pot of stories, emotions, experiences, and insights into my life.

Although, as a human, I am very much an individual, tales of joy, happiness, sadness, love, and loss are replicated all over the world, billions of times over.

I therefore hope that you, the reader, can connect with the words within this book, and take something positive away from it, even if that 'something' is a gentle reminder that you are not alone.

I thoroughly hope that you enjoy the book.

Adrian Young
December 2024

You Can Find…

I am a firm believer in hope, and in recent years I have attempted to transform myself from a 'glass half empty', to a 'glass half full' kind of person.

It's a struggle to overcome a certain way of thinking that has become ingrained within you, but in time, be it days, months, or even years, it *can* be achieved.

With hope in mind, I wrote this poem about how the world may seem daunting, uncomfortable, or even downright nasty at times, but we can overcome all of that if we focus our minds on hope of a brighter future.

Darkness casts a shadow on the wall
The sunshine doesn't filter in at all
Nothing seems to work, how'd you come to feel?
The light and dark to her is all that isn't real
Go cast your mind away, if only for a dream

There you will find, you're bursting at the seams

You can find love, you can find peace
You can find everything in between
You can find hope, you can find joy
You can find everything that you're looking for

Nightmares form a sense that's insecure
The dreams may fade, and yet you'll seek them more
Nothing seems to work, so how'd you come to see?
The ups and downs to her are the only things so real
Go open up your mind, if only for a while
There you will see, she's only putting on the style

You can find love, you can find peace
You can find everything in between
You can find hope, you can find joy
You can find everything that you're looking for

A Political Broadcast

Politics has never interested me. In fact, I would even go as far as to say that I *despise* politics.

My personal opinion is that the politicians we see in the media are all on-par with one another: they say whatever it is they need to say in order to get what they want, and they'll then go back on all they spouted at the drop of a hat.

I am far from being the only person lacking any form of trust in those who run my country.

In fact, in 2023, the Office for National Statistics concluded that 57% of Britons that were surveyed stated they have 'little or no trust' in the UK government or Parliament. A shocking 68% stated they have the same level of trust in the individual political parties.

A particular frustration of mine is how politicians often fail to answer simple questions that are put to them within interviews.

A recent study concluded that, of the politicians investigated, over a seven-year period, they only fully answered the questions presented to them 57% of the time.

This would be unacceptable in almost all job roles. Imagine being a teacher and only answering just over half of all pupils' questions. Insanity.

What I see is not what you see
But they may see what we can see
But if nobody can start to see
Then maybe it's all make believe
We'll put a spin on what they hear
But what they hear is there nor here
Let's shut them off from what they hear
Fuck 'em all, this is *my* career
Some may say we're out of touch
But what I don't touch is not worth much
For my mighty hands have all the power
To turn this crap into *my* gold dust
I'll avoid the question, without hesitation
Dodge the bullet about my infatuation
All I care for is *my* reputation
I don't give a shit about the new regulations
It may seem like the great debate
But things won't change, you're decades late
You all live in a fallen state
We aren't enemies, we're all just 'mates'

Never Be Alone

During late 2020, through to 2023, I was experiencing one of the most difficult times of my life.

Although I had been through periods of depression throughout adulthood, nothing had ever come close to the depths that my mind had fallen to at that time.

I felt in an almost sedated state during all of my waking hours, which became about eighteen to twenty hours a day, thanks to a prolonged period of insomnia.

I did not consume a full meal for almost six months, and I locked myself away in my office, rarely venturing beyond the boundaries of my home.

My saving grace throughout this entire period was undoubtedly my daughter, Amelie, who never failed to bring me happiness in the darkest of times.

As I began to fix myself, little by little, day by day, I started to gain my confidence back, and in doing so, I met someone who brought stability to my life. I suddenly did not wish to be alone anymore. I sought company and rediscovered myself as a person.

The vast improvement in my mental health allowed me to realise something that I had all but forgotten—as long as you have someone special in your life, whether that be a partner, child, sibling, or friend, you will *never* truly be alone.

Toni and her two daughters, Emily and Sophia, came along at just the right time. They gave me hope, support, and the love I needed, and I hope Amelie and I do the same for them.

Thinking of the things that you once thought
Picking up the route which you once walked
Loneliness may gather moss on stone
Because with me, you'll never be alone

Looking for the things you want to see
Wishing you were where you want to be
Emptiness is long, just like the roads
Because with me, you'll never be alone

You and I, we're like a rolling stone
You and I, we'll find our own way home
You and I, we're like a rolling stone
You and I will never be alone

You came along at just the right time
At the point where I had lost my mind
Although I felt that this world, I'd disowned

With you, I'll never be alone

All the grey skies turned my days to haze
In a world where nothing is okay
You picked me up and made my life my own
With you, I'll never be alone

You and I, we're like a rolling stone
You and I, we'll find our own way home
You and I, we're like a rolling stone
You and I, we'll find our own way home
As long as we are one, we're not alone

Kiss On Your Forehead

I remember the kiss on your forehead
It's as clear as the day it occurred
Our eyes contained all emotions
The situation was simply absurd
I acted so damn irrational
I never wanted you ever to leave
I've learnt all the ways I destroyed us
And now my heart is awake on my sleeve
I told you I loved you forever
You told me that you loved me too
As you turned, and you left for the last time
The last time that I got to kiss you

It's Getting Better

I have always found it much easier to write about events which affect me negatively.

When something saddens me, I often reach for a pen and write my thoughts, which have a tendency to naturally develop into a song or a poem.

When I experience happiness, I tend to just enjoy the moment and allow it to lift my spirits.

Recognising this trait within myself gave me the gentle nudge I needed to sit down and collate my thoughts about how my life holds so many positive factors; I have people in my life who love me, I have an incredible daughter, two amazing step-daughters, a partner who is also my best friend, and so much more to be thankful for.

Can you feel the sunshine warm your mind now?
Can you feel the music lift your soul?

Can you feel the love growing in your heart? Wow!
Can you feel the beat of the rock 'n' roll?

I can feel it taking over
I can feel it everywhere
It's getting better
(It's getting better for me)
It's getting better
(It's getting better for me)

Can you feel the wind blowing through your hair now?
Can you feel the words playing on your mind?
Can you feel the passion making you want more now?
Can you feel the warmth growing deep inside?

I can feel it taking over
I can feel it everywhere
It's getting better
(It's getting better for me)
It's getting better
(It's getting better for me)

Can you feel the sense of your belonging?
Can you feel the need to just want more?
Can you feel the desire to bring more songs in?
Can you feel the want to open all closed doors?

I can feel it taking over
I can feel it everywhere
It's getting better

(It's getting better for me)
It's getting better
(It's getting better for me)

Home Alone

So much time
Coming down self-abused
But it all means nothing
When you have very little to lose
Staying at home
Watching yourself waste away
Yet, it seems like heaven
When you've got nowhere else to stay

What have you got that's all worth fighting for?
What more can you need when you have it all?

Four walls
Closing in and squeezing
Nothing makes sense
There is no rhyme nor reason
Windows shut
You don't feel fresh air
The world passes by
Yet you don't seem to care

What have you got that's all worth fighting for?

What more can you need when you have it all?

Closed mind
You don't see any direction
As time passes by
There's nothing new to ever mention
You don't feel
There is an escape
From the clutches of your own mind
There's no mistake

What have you got that's all worth fighting for?
What more can you need when you have it all?

The Executioner

I gave you everything you ever wanted
I gave you all my world—is that enough?
I topped the world to see what I was doing
Looking down there, all I saw was us

Every time I dream, it all falls down
Breaking up like everything I do
The executioner sits beside my heart
Removes the mask, and standing there is you

You don't realise the things I'm thinking
My mind is spinning up and round the room
My knees are weak, my soul is simply crawling
My eyes can't see what's going to happen soon

Every time I dream, it all falls down
Breaking up like everything I do
The executioner sits beside my heart
Removes the mask, and standing there is you

Here we go, what do I do?
Do I just stand up and walk away from you?

I'm in a mindset, I have to believe
That what I will choose now, is what I want to see

Every time I dream, it all falls down
Breaking up like everything I do
The executioner sits beside my heart
Removes the mask, and standing there is you

Burning Bridges

In recent years, I have frequented many open mic nights within my hometown and surrounding area.

Such events are an opportunity for musicians, poets, story-tellers and the like to perform in front of a live audience and lay the foundations of their craft.

At one such event, in January 2023, I watched a gentleman by the name of Sean Clack, who I had previously seen perform his own songs.

With a musical itch to scratch, I asked Sean if I could sing with him on one of his own compositions.

As we performed together, we soon realised that our vocal tones and styling complemented one another, so we agreed to meet at a later date and share ideas, and perhaps write some songs together.

Upon our first meeting, Sean introduced an idea for a song about 'burning bridges', which spoke of moving on from the past. Thirty minutes later, this became our first co-written composition.

Looking back at the fires
That were started between you and me
But time has rolled on
And I know we've got so much to see

Are we way past turning back
To where we were and what we had?
Is it too late, as I state the facts?

As we watch our bridges burn
Surely there are lessons to learn
Could we save what we had
And then we can build stronger back

Can we dampen the fires
That rage high between you and me?
Deep down inside, I know that you agree

Can we rebuild the bridges between you and me
Before it's too late to come back
From the brink of losing what we once had?

Can we rebuild the bridges between you and me
Before it's too late, and our dreams have turned to ash?

Break Down

You're so caught up in your busy life
Too much to do and not enough time
I bet you don't even go out at night
You just sit alone and cry

You're so worried about how you look
You'll never break the rules, you're misunderstood
I bet you've never even been in love
You just keep it all inside

Don't just break down
Please, don't just break down
All over again

You're so full of wise remarks
Life to you is just a shot in the dark
I bet you don't even dream at night
You just lay alone and cry

You're all made up like you're something new
Lost in your own mind, with nothing to do
I bet you've never even smiled today

You just hide it all inside

Don't just break down
Please, don't just break down
All over again

Blue-Eyed, Blonde-Haired Lover

There's newspapers all strewn
Across my bathroom floor
There are words of love and hate in paint
Across my new front door
I think I have it summed up
In my own philosophy
My blue-eyed, blonde-haired lover
She isn't coming back to me

She's had too much of my foolish games
I run around like 'Jack-the-lad', as I'm driving her insane

Well, I woke up on the floor
Whilst my head was in the clouds
The banging in my head
Is getting far too, much too loud
As I focus on surroundings
Whilst last night is a haze
My blue-eyed, blonde-haired lover

She isn't coming back for days

She's had too much of my foolish games
I run around with no control, it's me she can't sustain

So everybody tells me
That last night had become
Something of a nightmare
That resembled hell for some
Starts with good intentions
It all ends in blazing rows
My blue-eyed, blonde-haired lover
Had left running out of the house

She's had too much of my foolish games
I run around and drive her mad, so I'm the one to blame

Caught in a Haze

※ ※ ※

As someone who has battled anxiety and depression all my life, a sense of being trapped is a familiar feeling to me.

Sometimes life has made me feel suffocated; my chest tightens, my throat closes up, my head feels like it's held within a vice, which continuously tightens until the discomfort becomes too much.

'Caught in a Haze' is a small time capsule of such emotions, which may provide you the slightest insight into my mind when it becomes troubled.

※ ※ ※

I'm trapped in a bubble, and nothing will burst
I band-aide the bleeding, but the wound still hurts
I'm stuck in a locked room—I can't find the key
I open up my closed eyes, but I still cannot see
My head's in the clouds, caught in the wind
I try to be a good soul, but my heart's full of sin

I'm caught in a haze
I'm truly caught in a haze

Well, life's little mazes are driving me crazy
And I'm losing my mind again
I can't seem to sleep or stand on my feet
I'm going right round the bend
But I'm coming back, get my life right back on track
Getting straight to my old ways, breaking out of the haze

I'm caught in a haze
I'm really caught in a haze

I'm lost on a highway, can't read the map
Stuck in a reserve between this and that
I'm trapped in a rat race, which I can't seem to win
So, I keep on running, but I'm all out of steam
I'm locked in a crossfire, can't avoid the shots
I feel like I'm in reload, with the firing pin cocked

I'm caught in a haze
Forever caught in a haze

Acting the Fool

In 1955, Lonnie Donegan released a song which changed the entire direction of popular music.

'Rock Island Line', believed to have been originally composed by Clarence Wilson in 1929, took the United Kingdom by storm, and resulted in the creation of countless 'skiffle' bands.

A young John Lennon fronted one such group, which would eventually lead to the formation of The Beatles.

Just like 'Rock Island Line', there are endless songs from all around the globe which have been penned on the timeless format of train travel, and it was this which inspired me to write 'Acting the Fool'.

It tells the fictional story of someone returning home to the person they love, after making regrettable mistakes, only to end the situation in the most unpleasant of ways.

Standing on the platform of the train station
Waiting for my ride to come take me away
Standing with my ticket, I can't wait to leave
This time, in my mind, I'll wait for another day

I board the carriage, wait for my home town
Try not to doze off as my mind wanders away
Thinking thoughts of homeland and the open sky
Can't wait to get there and I sure as hell will stay

What to do and what to say is such a question
I'll pay the price for always acting a fool
I know I'll slip, and I will often stumble
The truth of the matter is I'll always lose

And so I get home, I can't wait to lay
Beside the girl that is my only one
And as she slides her fingers through my hair
My hand will reach for my lonely gun

So, the day comes where she'll meet her maker
I was laying down right by her side
Her final words, I shall never surrender
Right before I put a bullet right in her eye

What to do and what to say is such a question

I'll pay the price for always acting a fool
I know I'll slip, and I will often stumble
The truth of the matter is I'll always lose

What Makes a Man?

During the early part of 2023, whilst trawling through the endless pit of (often) useless information which we call Facebook, I came across a post by a gentleman with whom I attended school.

Thom Bailey was always interested in the arts for as long as I can remember, with a keen interest in film and acting.

Throughout our early teens, Thom and I would discuss recent cinema releases, with one example being Wes Craven's slasher horror *Scream*, which was released in 1996.

We were only eleven years old at its time of release, but we watched it many times, and became huge fans.

Our passion even reached the point whereby we filmed our own horror, captured in all its glory on a handheld camcorder.

It came as no surprise when Thom's Facebook post advertised the fact his dream had become a reality and he had opened his own theatre.

Excitedly, I messaged Thom in order to congratulate him, and I planted the seed that would ultimately lead to the writing of this, and many other compositions. I advised Thom that should he ever wish to host a musical production, I would be interested in becoming involved. I further advised him I also had many contacts within the local music scene, who would be very interested in such projects.

Many months later, Thom and I met, and I proposed an idea which was inspired by *This Girl*—a small theatre production I had seen whilst visiting Liverpool.

The play told the story of Cynthia Powell, who fell in love with a fellow college student named John Lennon.

The play was based around a series of songs, most of which were original compositions, performed live by the cast.

I began brainstorming ideas for a show, which would allow me to advance my writing skills, and make use of the songs I had been composing throughout adulthood.

The premise of the show would revolve around two males within our local area, and the difficulties they faced whilst growing up.

During my research, the very first article I read was entitled 'What Makes a Man?'. My attention was immediately captured, and I set about writing a song to address that very question.

Although that production never came to fruition, I have continued to write a play which I hope to develop into a stage production in the near-future.

When I was young, my daddy said,
'One day, you'll have to be strong,
Life will throw its challenges;
you must know right from wrong'

Tell me, what makes a man?
Is it someone who does all they can?
Tell me, what makes a man?
Is it someone who'll hold your hand?

When times get hard, too hard for living
You get nowhere and life's unforgiving
If you need love, you can turn to him
No matter how hard, he will never give in
Is this what makes a man?

The world seems to want all she can take
There's no time for rest
The pressure mounts, the stress will build
You've got to be one of the best

Tell me, what makes a man?
Is it someone who does all they can?
Tell me, what makes a man?
Is it someone who'll hold your hand?

When times get hard, too hard for living
You get nowhere and life's unforgiving
If you need love, you can turn to him
No matter how hard, he will never give in
Is this what makes a man?

Hold your head up, don't you cry
There is no room for tears
You're the rock—the building block
You must set aside all your fears

Is this what makes a man?

Break Me Down/Lift Me Up

❖⟫ ⋯ ✦ ⋯ ⟪❖

In *My Verses* I touched upon religion, and how, from a young age, I have always questioned my beliefs.

Since that time, I have become much more self-aware and in-tune with my faith.

As someone who attends a very musical church, with regular live music performed by a band, I often draw inspiration from those songs, which filter into my writing.

'Break Me Down/Lift Me Up' explores the idea of having to reach your lowest possible point, in order to realise how much you can truly raise yourself back up again.

Within my life, I have been lower than I ever imagined was possible, but I overcame every obstacle, and arrived at the other end a better person than I had ever been before.

A large part of my recovery was thanks to my faith.

❖⟫ ⋯ ✦ ⋯ ⟪❖

Lord, please forgive me

I'm confessing all my sins
I have a whole host of regrets
I'm forgetting everything
I'm down on my knees, begging, please
Show me the righteous way
I want to break free from these strong winds
And cast my past away

Break me down to a place I don't know
Break me down, far away, where they don't go
(Because) I can't see what I should see
Times ticking away from me
Everything feels like make believe
Nothing is ever what it seems

Sha la la la, la la la la, things will be all right
Sha la la la, la la la la, the days are getting bright

I waded in the river
Washed my blues away
Hung my head for the holy cross
Then prayed away my days
Recited all the verses
As I looked up at the sky
But nothing seems to cut it
And I have no idea why

Lift me up to a place I don't know
Lift me up, far away, where they don't go
I can't see what I should see

Times ticking away from me
Everything feels make believe
Nothing is ever what it seems

Sha la la la, la la la la, things will be all right
Sha la la la, la la la la, the days are getting bright

Wherever You Go

Sometimes in life, we feel that our problems just seem to follow us around.

No matter how hard we try to deal with life's issues, we can't seem to run quick enough in order to get away from the problems we often face.

'Wherever You Go' is based upon this premise.

You think about the times
When you know you crossed the line
You've never, ever, felt like this before

Your eyes don't see the world
Your heart doesn't know you've turned
Into something that just isn't you

When you're sitting, waiting, wishing

That the whole world will wait for you
You're thinking that you feel love
Your problems follow you wherever you go

You think about the times
When you know you crossed the line
You've never, ever felt like this before

Your eyes don't see the world
Your heart doesn't know you've turned
Into something that just isn't you

When you're sitting, waiting, wishing
That the whole world will wait for you
You're thinking that you feel love
Your problems follow you wherever you go

Time waits for no man
This, that, the other, it's all the same
Wading through the water
Here, there and everywhere
We are all to blame

Flying

⋅»⋅⋅♦⋅⋅«⋅

There are times when I write in order to release some emotions, but may not know what I am trying to say, or why. 'Flying' was one such moment.

The words just spilled out of me as though they were a weight upon my shoulders that needed lifting.

When I read the words back to myself, I felt as though I was subconsciously addressing mistakes I have made in the past.

Perhaps I was seeking something that I already had right in front of me.

⋅»⋅⋅♦⋅⋅«⋅

I was flying too close to the sun
Man, that thing shines upon
Everything in the world, but you and me

I was flying too close to the moon

Man, that thing went too soon
It may never cast a shadow on you and me

You and I, together, we've been through wars
But you know that we've come through the other side
No matter what happens, you're the one I adore
You and I, together, forever more

We're flying high, to touch the sky
We're flying high, just you and I

I was flying too close to the stars
Man, those things show my scars
They will never expose you and me

I was flying too close to the clouds
It feels like I'm floating now
Maybe we could find the ninth, you and me

You and I, together, we've been through wars
But you know that we've come through the other side
No matter what happens, you're the one I adore
You and I, together, forever more

We're flying high, to touch the sky
We're flying high, just you and I

Covertly Caring

Within *My Verses*, 'Long Road Home' told the story of how I felt after the passing of my step-dad, Robert Charles Dyble.

Also inspired by Robert's passing, 'Covertly Caring' is about his perspective during the last period of his life.

We, as a family, knew that he didn't want us to suffer with him. He knew he was dying, and he believed he would not make it through his illness.

He told no one, other than my dad, what he believed his fate to be.

Forever the gentle soul, and wanting to protect us all from further pain, he kept his fear hidden away.

I think you know it all
But you just won't say
Like a bird, I'll fly far away

Just to get above everything I hate
It is my escape just to fly away

It's only natural just to want to hide
Just to slip away under a new disguise
And to hide my face, hide that I'm not all right
Because to face the truth is better than to lie
..in your arms, you're my lucky charm
You're the one
Won't you please hold me tight?
Tell me all is all right, then we're done

You think you've seen it all, but the world's gone dark
Bet you want to talk, but it's just too fast
Take in a breath, then let out a sigh
Because to face the past is better than to lie
..in your arms, you're my lucky charm
You're the one
Won't you please hold me tight?
Tell me all is all right, then we're done

High and Mighty

High and mighty girl, she thinks she knows it all
She's better than me, she's better than us all
She comes in creeping, peeping, kind of 'walking the line'
She thinks she has it all, but not this time

She thinks she knows how the other half lives
You better believe it, because this is it
She comes, she goes, but she never gives
You better believe it, because this is it

She won't let you digress it, nor catch you when you fall
You can get in deep, but your life is a crawl
If you're gonna consider if it turns out fine
When you're pushing forward, but she leaves you behind

Time's a healer, can't you see?
This is not the way it's supposed to be
Sitting alone, like me, without her

She's Left Home

Hindsight is a wonderful thing. We all do and say things we may not mean, but we certainly live to regret some choices we make.

Some decisions can lead to immense loss, and you don't know what you've got until you lose it, and that can certainly be true for relationships.

We, as humans, can be susceptible to pushing others away, and it isn't until they are pushed enough to leave that we realise what a lonely place the world can suddenly become.

I'm off to see my baby
To make sure she's all right
If she doesn't have the feelings
Then I'll give her some tonight
Because to me it doesn't matter

If she's wrong or if I'm right
So, I'm going to see my baby
I'm going to make things right tonight

Oh no, she's left home
Oh no, she's got no place to go
I've got a funny feeling
That she's going out of sight
So, I'm going to see my baby
I'm going to make things right tonight

I'm searching in the shadows
Whilst I'm running down the road
Got to find my one and only
No, she shouldn't be alone
Because these streets she's walking
Are not safe for
An empty little heart
When she's lying on the floor

The night is getting long
The day is getting old
I'm starting to lose my mind
Trying to find this lonely soul
She doesn't even care
When her heart grows cold
I'm going to see my baby
And the truth be told

Oh no, she's left home

Oh no, she's got no place to go
I've got the strangest feeling
Like she's going out of sight
So, I'm going to see my baby
I'm going to make things right tonight

Stupid Cupid

◆)) · ·◆· ·((◆

Love, or more specifically, being in love, is something I have always battled with.

I have always been unable to define what it means to *be in love*. How do I know if I'm in love? How would anyone know they were in love with me?

There have been times when I feel Cupid has been toying with me—giving me love only to take it away.

This thought process lead me to recollect Martin Luther's phrase, 'What the right hand gives, the left hand takes', which then grew into this song.

The title stems from a song I had been listening to since my early teens, namely 'Stupid Cupid', by Connie Francis (1958).

◆)) · ·◆· ·((◆

Stupid Cupid, stop messing around
I've had enough of that beautiful sound you call a voice

Oh yeah, it's *such* a voice

Stupid Cupid, you've lost your sense
I've had enough of your arguments, it's getting late
Oh yeah, it's getting late

I hope in the morning it will be all right
Why do you always have to put up such a fight?
And I know that you won't be hanging around
Stupid Cupid, why don't you just back on down?

Stupid Cupid, you've lost your nerve
You fall apart like I know you deserve; you got away
Oh yeah, you got away

Stupid Cupid, stop pickin' on me
You leave a lonely heart to bleed, you're here to stay
Oh yeah, you're here to stay

I know in the morning it will be all right
Why do you always have to put up such a fight?
And I know that you won't be hanging around
Stupid Cupid, why don't you just back on down?

Stupid Cupid, your left hand gives
Your right hand takes and it's causing a rift, I need a break
Oh yeah, I need a break

I pray in the morning it will be all right
Why do you have to give me such a fright?

Yes, I know that you won't be hanging around
Stupid Cupid, why don't you just back on down?

The Day We Left

In the middle of the morning
Or last thing at night
I have to follow my feelings
I've got to do what feels right
Because the last time I left you
I was left standing blue
In the middle of the morning
The last time I left you

Time is a healer
So, you better watch your step
Time will run away from you
Don't you live with those regrets
Don't waste your life just fooling around
And chasing dreams
Looking back, regretting
The day that you left me

I'm left with the shadows
Of the past growing old
My fortune favours regret
Or so I have been told

And in the night time, or the daylight
It doesn't matter if it feels right
I've got to do what I feel is true
Every time that I leave you

Time is a healer
So, you better watch your step
Time will run away from you
Don't you live with those regrets
Don't waste your life just fooling around
And chasing dreams
Looking back, regretting
The day that you left me

These Days

These days are always hard days
And it seems like they're fading away
Singing songs to lonely crowds
This is not tomorrow, this is now

Whilst you sit around wondering
What life can sometimes bring
I walk away into another day
I turn my head, and this is what I say:

'It's all right now
The times are changing, and I've discovered how
It's all right now
I'm looking forward, it's looking brighter now'

I wonder where the years have gone
It seems that I've got to carry on
Whilst I look back and wonder how
I'll forget tomorrow, this is now

And while you sit around pondering
What life can always bring

I walk away into another day
I turn my head, and this is what I say:

'All we know
Is that this life takes its toll
It winds me up
And it tears apart my soul'

It's all right now
The times are changing, and I've discovered how
Yes, it's all right now
I'm looking forward, it's looking brighter now

Banned

We should ban speech, but talk it all through
We should ban breathing, but gasp when they do
We should ban music, then sing whilst we dance
We should ban warnings, but advise them in advance
We should ban jokes, because that may seem funny
We should ban cash, but pay for the pleasure with money
We should ban opinions, but disclose how we feel
We should ban A.I., but let's not forget what is real
We should ban banning, but that may highlight
The tediously tedious altering of life

Yesterday's Another Day

He can't wait long just to hear what you are singing
He can't close his ears
Whilst you bang the bell you're ringing
He must have been caught in the trap you were preparing
Because yesterday's another day

He won't smile at your jokes or make you feel better, baby
Tuck you in at night when you feel like being lazy
Give you medication when you think you're going crazy
Because yesterday's another day

It's all you feel
It's all you know
These things are real
Yesterday's another day
Didn't you know?

He won't sing you a song, he'll make you feel like a martyr
Cross his little heart, promise that he'll try harder

You're lucky that the gun he got is just a little starter
Because yesterday's another day

You double cross your fingers
In the hope that he will change
More than desperation that you'll see some better days
I won't hold your breath
That the prick will change his ways
Because yesterday's another day

The last time he hit you, well, he said it was the last
He said the person who he was is faded in the past
He took to your face like lightning to a mast
Because yesterday's another day

So, what will it take to make you finally walk away?
A dagger in your heart will beat a beating every day
Does it really matter what we think or what you say?
Because yesterday's another day

Us and the World

⋙ ⋅⋅✦⋅⋅ ⋘

Imagine being sat in your home, alone, in a space which used to be full of happiness and laughter.

What once was a place of joy, safety, and smiles, is now a place of regret, silence and sadness.

⋙ ⋅⋅✦⋅⋅ ⋘

When you feel all alone
And your love's not coming home
It's like an old dream, fading away

When you seem to get it wrong
And all your love has simply gone
It's like an old road, going nowhere

You don't seem to feel the way I do
You don't seem to see the things I want you to
So, let's go back to how we were

In the old days, us and the world

When you look so down
Your feet don't touch the ground
It's like a life race, you'll never win

When you say these things
Act like you'll never win
It's like emotions will bring you down

You don't seem to feel the way I do
You don't seem to see the things I want you to
So, let's go back to how we were
In the old days, us and the world

Yes, let's go back to how we were
In the old days, us and the world

Watch It All Go Wrong

⇢ ‧ ♦ ‧ ⇠

Have you ever held down a job that fills you with misery? So many of us have, and it's very unpleasant.

What can further exacerbate an unpleasant workplace is an equally unpleasant management 'team'.

Sadly, there is a segment of society who, when they progress their career and hold a level of power within their workplace, turn their backs on friends, become bullies, and ultimately become very vexatious.

Ultimately, we are all often trying to achieve the same goals when we work; to earn money, support our families, and live a fruitful life.

Therefore, it's important we support one another, rather than turn against one another.

⇢ ‧ ♦ ‧ ⇠

Who made the rule
That you can't smile because you're happy?

When you know every day
That you're only trying to get by
So, they're bringing you down
When you're voicing your opinions
You should know by now
That your life is set in stone

So, you see, boy, I told you all along
Take a seat, and watch it all go wrong

Time after time they make you scream
Man, my mind is gone
It's bringing you down
Deep inside, you know there's no way out
You look over your shoulder
Searching for times to decide
To leave now or later
When you know you're locked down tight

So, you see, boy, I told you all along
Take a seat, and watch it all go wrong

I turn a blind eye
And I pray that the day may end soon
My mind is numbed
By the thoughts that tomorrow may come
I'm cold to the core
My eyes are wide to the truth now
The sooner I break myself free
The sooner my soul can breathe

So, you see, boy, I told you all along
Take a seat, and watch it all go wrong

Won't Fade Away

Flowers don't always seem to grow in your hair
Sunshine won't shine on the things you live to regret
There's a storm that builds in your mind
All of the time
But it won't fade away

Smiles don't seem to grow, you fight back the tears
The things that you grew up to love, grow into fears
There's a rage in your heart
That fights like a fading star
But it won't fade away

Your hope doesn't seem to grow directly home
Because happiness is just a fortunate perk of the soul
There's a pain in your eyes
That pulls at the strings of my heart
But it won't fade away
No, it won't fade away

You Can't Fool Me

You draw attention to yourself
The spotlight is bright
And it's bad for your health
If it's attention you want, yeah, you'll get it for free

The curtains are closed and the night's drawing in
All the doors they are locked, so confess all your sins
If it's forgiveness you want
You may get it, but not from me

All the places I've been, all the things that I've seen
All the people I meet on the dirty old street
All the looks in their eyes, all the self-pity lies
But you can't fool me; no you can't fool me, anymore

You asked to be heard, so you shouted out loud
I can see in your eyes you are nothing but proud
If it's praise that you seek
You see, you'll never be free

Because you won't walk on water or turn it into wine
Your shit life is that, and you'll never be fine

If there are things you want
You won't get it if it's up to me

All the places I've been, all the things that I've seen
All the people I meet on the dirty old street
All the looks in their eyes, all the self-pity lies
But you can't fool me; no you can't fool me, anymore

What Is the Difference?

What is the difference between poems and songs?
Is it the place within your heart in which they belong?
What is the difference between you and I?
It seems that may change in the blink of an eye
What is the difference between love and hate?
Is it the words that you say, or the pain you create?
What is the difference between right and wrong?
Is it subjective, whilst dividing the weak from the strong?
What is the difference when all's said and done
When you're looking right down the barrel of a gun?

Bumpy Ride

Whilst sat at home one evening, I received a text message from Toni, a friend, who would later become my partner.

Explaining how she found herself in a low mood, it became apparent Toni had been reading my first book, *My Verses*. She stated that she wished for her to be the subject of some of the poetry about love.

In my attempt at making her feel better, I told Toni that those tough times will soon pass, and that tomorrow *is* another day.

The conversation got me thinking that life can sure be a bumpy ride at times.

You've been running wild, trying to stand
Jettison feelings with a helping hand
Collecting thoughts, when you struggle to cope
Whilst the rest of the world dissipates your hope

So, come on baby, don't you feel blue
This old world will never defeat you
Keep your chin up, hold on tight
This may be a bumpy ride

Time will tell if what you're waiting for
Is on the other side of a padlocked door
Grasp what you love, forget what you hate
'cause this old life will always whittle away

So, come on baby, don't you feel blue
This old world will never forget you
Keep your chin up, hold on tight
This may be a bumpy ride

This life breaks us down
When you feel like there's no way out
Yet, I know there's always hope
I just pray that you feel it so

So, come on baby, don't you feel blue
This old world will never defeat you
Keep your chin up, hold on tight
This may be a bumpy ride

Playing Games

❖❖──◆──❖❖

'Point scoring' may, to most, be a phrase we are most likely to use when discussing sports, but the common phrase can often have negative connotations.

Relationships, of any kind, may likely have their difficulties, and when the situation becomes fragile, we may resort to 'point scoring'.

Common arguments that we throw around may include 'You did X, so I did Y', and 'You said A, so I'm telling you B'.

Sometimes, we simply want to have the last word in an argument, and it all becomes somewhat of an unpleasant game.

❖❖──◆──❖❖

I wake up in the morning and my heart kind of cries
But you're never going to break me
I can see through your lies

You're like a wrecking ball, you'll break me in all ways
But I just won't play your games

I'm going to start again and step upon a building block
I haven't seen you much, but I feel that you'll never stop
You're just like a hologram, we're all the same
But I just won't play your games

I'm looking at reflections and I don't mind looking back
Picking out the holes when the light has gone
It's all turned to black
When everything has gone and nothing but you remained
But we still keep playing those games

It might seem funny and it may seem a kind of strange
It may be a struggle for you to contemplate
But we both know things will never be the same again
For as long as we play these games

Here I Go Again

Here I go again
Running 'round in circles since I don't know when
I've been up, I've been down
I've been lost, and I've been found

Yet I'm still so confused
What do I even do when it comes back 'round to you?
When you say you don't want me no more
You'll always find a way
Of knocking right back at my door

I am so afraid of being alone
No, I never want to be on my own

Tell me more, tell me less
Is it something that I know
Or something that I have to guess?
This is why in my mind
My head's in a total state of distress

I am so afraid of being alone
No, I never want to be on my own

Are you just playing games?
It's like we're running 'round in circles
And you're messing with my brain
Here I stand, so confused
Just look right at my face and tell me, do I look amused?

I am so afraid of being alone
No, I never want to be on my own

I Don't Want War

I often write in a way in which the context isn't necessarily obvious.

The style is interesting to me, and it allows for a story to be told regarding what the lyrics mean. It also allows the reader an opportunity to contextualize the words in whichever way their own thought processes allow.

One such poem is 'I Don't Want War'.

This poem is my personal expressionism of a particular element in life that we all have to face from time to time.

The lyrics are open to interpretation, and the fact we all see things differently is part of the beauty of art, and life.

Well, we've seen it all before
And I'm sure we'll meet again
When you're closing all the doors
And you'll dispose of all the men

They all seem to be running
'till they finally hit the wall
Lord, I know we see them coming
But they never seem to fall

I don't war, because I'll never feel true
I don't want war, if it means I'm losing you
We've got to stand like we never did before
I don't want war

I'm chasing all the shadows
I swear I always seem to find
The picture's turning narrow
And our love is always blind

I don't war, because I'll never feel true
I don't want war, if it means I'm losing you
We've got to stand like we never did before
I don't want war

Senses

I can feel the sunshine warming me
I can feel the gentle, cooling breeze
I can feel the rain drops bearing down
I can feel the snowflakes freeze the air
I can feel the winter wind to bear
I can feel the cold seep deep inside
All I want to feel is your love

I can see the heartache all around
I can see the mad ones running around
I can see the losing of your mind
I can see the sure signs of the times
I can see the way in which your love is blind
I can see there's never no going back
All I want to see is your love

I can hear the things that you wish to say
I can hear the words in the wind whirl away
I can hear the pain in the sound of your voice
I can hear what you really mean when you lie
I can hear the song that you sing when you sigh
I can hear your breath gently touching my soul

All I want to hear is your love
All I want to see is your love
All I want to feel is your love
All I ever need is your love

Yesterday

Looking at the sun, peering at the moon
Watching the crow flying away too soon
Feeling the grass on the tips of my toes
Where my footsteps lead me, well, nobody knows

So, I can say I'm feeling better today
Than I ever did yesterday
The sun shines brighter, everything's good
In each and every way
I never want to relive yesterday

The stars seem brighter in the nighttime sky
It all seems warmer and I don't know why
I raise up my hands and sing to my God
As he fills me with love, with a wink and a nod

So, I can say I'm feeling better today
Than I ever did yesterday
The sun shines brighter, everything's good
In each and every way
I never want to relive yesterday

My hair floats alive in the summer breeze
This life seems lightweight, and I walk it with ease
My soul is alive and surrounded by smiles
I could get used to this, if just for a while

So, I can say I'm feeling better today
Than I ever did yesterday
The sun shines brighter, everything's good
In each and every way
I never want to relive yesterday

The darker clouds that formed
Have all but faded away
All the shadows that followed me
Are no longer welcome to stay
I am free, with a push and a pull
A shove just to keep them at bay
I never want to relive yesterday

I never want to relive yesterday
No, I never want to relive yesterday
I'll never, ever relive yesterday
No, I never want to relive yesterday

Sidewalk

December 8, 1980, brought one of the most shocking celebrity news stories into the living rooms of the entire world.

Whilst walking from his limousine, into the entrance of the Dakota building, just a stone's throw from New York's Central Park, a deranged fan shot John Lennon multiple times. John was pronounced dead a short time later.

The world was in mourning, whilst trying to come to terms with the shock of such an unprecedented event.

Who, and more to the point, *why*, would someone kill a man who brought so much joy to so many people?

I have been a fan of The Beatles since 2001, when I discovered their music at the tender age of 16.

Just like so many before me, I've grown to know the band's lives and history on a granular level.

Forty-three years after the fact, I still find it shocking and painful when I think about John's murder.

During September 2022, I visited New York for the first time. I always dreamt of visiting such an incredible city, and it absolutely captivated me.

Whilst there, I visited the Dakota, in all its gothic beauty.

For a considerable time, I simply stood where John was shot.

I thought about the suffering he and his wife, Yoko Ono, must have felt, both physically and emotionally.

I thought about John's sons, Julian and Sean, along with the anger and deep-rooted sadness which must still reverberate within them today.

More than anything else, I felt an overwhelming sadness at how this world can be so brutal and cruel.

Take a midnight walk
Take a hold of me
Step along the walkway
Don't look back to see

Hear the rings of fire
Feel them crashing down
Under cover of the moonlight
With no one around

It's a night to remember
One we'd rather forget
In the middle of a sidewalk
Where the great man's dead

In the back of your mind
All the fears come true
Sing a song to remember
Until the day is through

Line the streets of New York
Fill the garden, too
Hold his heart in your hands
There's nothing we can do

It's a night to remember
One we'd rather forget
In the middle of a sidewalk
Where the great man's dead

It's a night to remember
One we'd sooner forget
In the middle of a sidewalk
Where John lays dead

You Should Know

I was young, quite the fool
I didn't know just what to do
I'd always hoped I'd grow old with you

So naïve, I missed the point
I grew a heart that's so mis-joined
I didn't know the way, that is true

Time says you've lost your mind
You can't go through this all the time
I know what you're thinking, my dear friend
This thing called love will condescend your soul
But you should know

The days are gone; the nights are dead
I can't forgive all that I said
Just a sleepy town in my mind

The dreams may fade, the hope may fall
You'll be there in no time at all
Looking for the feeling you may find

Time says you've lost your mind
You can't go through this all the time
I know what you're thinking, my dear friend
This thing called love will condescend your soul
But you should know
Yes, you should know
We all should know
We all grow old

Time Flies Away

As we grow into adulthood, the protective fields we receive from parents — a loving home environment, education, and a lack of financial commitments — often protect most of us from the challenges of adulthood.

As we travel through life, we experience loss, parenthood, financial troubles, and many more elements of which we have no choice other than to navigate.

I was no longer a child when I first experienced the death of a loved one, but, naturally, the older I become, the more I experience grief.

With such a whirlwind of emotions we often have around us, we soon understand how temporary life may be for some, and how quickly time can simply pass us by.

Just when you think it's over, it's only just begun
One thing to another, I'm loaded like a gun

The end of a long road, which ways have I gone?
It feels like a lifetime, I'm losing everyone

Time flies away, there's nothing left to say
Who's in your way when time flies away?

Lonely like a lost soul, but free as a bird
Screaming out in silence, when nothing's ever heard

The minutes fade to hours, the days slide away
The light turns to darkness, and there it shall stay

Time flies away, there's nothing left to say
Who's in your way when time flies away?

If you'd ever told me that this life fades to dust
I'd likely laugh about it, as I rot away to rust
Now I am older, I never waste the days
I'll always come out smiling, even when time fades away

Time flies away, there's nothing left to say
Who's here to stay when time flies away?

The Best Is Yet to Be

Say goodbye to yesterday
Turn your back, learn to walk away
Now I know I can finally see
The truth of the matter is the best is yet to be

Learn to love, forget to hate
Turn a blind eye to all your mistakes
Now I know, I can finally leave
The truth of the matter is the best is yet to be

Don't resent those you appreciate
Turn it round and emancipate
Now I know what I should believe
The truth of the matter is the best is yet to be

I can't afford not to love
I can't afford to leave
Lord, won't you help me see
That the best is yet to be

Dream

We're pulling in all directions
And nothing is what it seems
We've lost all sense of balance
This reality's but a dream

Time to Go

Come on, baby, take my hand
Let's go walking in a foreign land
We'll climb aboard that Greyhound bus
Making tracks and kicking up a fuss

Start a voyage of self-discovery
Nothing else matters, other than you and me
Ripping up maps whilst we're finding us
Breaking locks and building up trust

Close your senses and learn to feel
We'll fly the highway where nothing is real
Hand in your pocket, ticking up time
Pushing boundaries and finding the line

Hold your breath
See how you feel on the other side
There's no time for rest
Pack your bags because it's time to go

Guilty Hill

I've got blood on my hands and it's making me ill
I never left my love and no, I never will
She knows how to make me rock and roll
She is only ever seemingly out of control
She just left me hanging by the silvery moon
Left me on my lonesome, on top' Guilty Hill

I've got soles on my shoes and they're helping me walk
Down the hill and through the open door
I know how to make myself revolve
Steer away from trouble—I will not get involved
I've just been left by the silvery moon
Standing on my lonesome, on top' Guilty Hill

See my feelings
See my hurt
She's pushing me down into my own graves dirt
See my misery
See my pain
I'm not going through the same thing again

She's got money to spend and a house to boot

Up the driveway, onto Guilty Hill
She knows how to make me doubt myself
Make me feel guilty for just being myself
She's got me on my knees, begging with all my will
Kick me in the face and throw me down Guilty Hill

See my feelings
See my hurt
She's pushing me down into my own graves dirt
See my misery
See my pain
I'm not going through the same thing again

Millionaire (Better With You)

For me, writing about sadness has always been much easier than writing about joy.

I'm not entirely sure why this is the case, but I can pick up my guitar at any moment in the day and write sad sounding songs that speak of loss and pain. Yet, if I attempt to write a song of joy, it seems much harder to find the right words or melody.

'Millionaire (Better With You)' captures one of those moments where the words just seemed to flow.

It tells the story of the pure elation that one feels when that 'special someone' is in their lives, and, thanks to them, everything is a million times better.

This song is another example of co-writing, where the chorus was brought to me as the song's foundation, and I built the rest of the song around the original idea.

I've got a million reasons to be happy
I've got a million reasons not to feel blue
I've got a million reasons why my life's so much better
Yeah, it's so much better with you

You turn the grey skies from dark to blue
It feels like there's nothing we can't do
I feel so lucky that I'm your man
If we can't do it, then nobody can

I've got a million reasons to be happy
I've got a million reasons not to feel blue
I've got a million reasons, my life's so much better
Yeah, it's so much better with you

They say money can't buy you love
But you and me, baby, we sure bought enough
When you hold my hand and squeeze
You tell me that I'm the 'one you need'

I've got a million reasons to be happy
I've got a million reasons not to feel blue
I've got a million reasons, my life's so much better
Yeah, it's so much better with you

Life's a journey and I want to take it with you

So many twists and turns, but, baby, we'll pull through
We'll always pull through
That's what we're going to do

I've got a million reasons to be happy
I've got a million reasons not to feel blue
I've got a million reasons, my life's so much better
Yeah, it's so much better with you
It's always so much better with you

Never Easy

In contrast to the last song, 'Never Easy' captures one of those solemn moments, where the art of writing naturally became a method of escapism, capturing my mindset within the moment, akin to a photograph capturing a split second in time.

I feel life's too much
Nothing comes out easy
Sometimes things get rough
Nothing seems to please me
I bow down my head
Close my eyes and think of home
Nothing's ever left unsaid
Sat in silence, all alone

The best is never easy

When you don't even believe in yourself
I know I'll always need me
I'll forever believe in myself

No, this life is never easy

I feel emptiness
Nothing makes me feel whole
Sometimes loneliness
May become my only goal
I lay upon my bed
Eyes wide, constant drone
Nothing's ever dead
Live forever, all alone

The best is never easy
When you don't even believe in yourself
I know I'll always need me
I'll forever believe in myself

No, this life is never easy

Save Me

One of the most joyous elements of writing, for me, are those moments when the words just flow out, one after another, in quick succession.

The words can be so personal, and self-reflective, that you know the context already. It then becomes natural to express yourself through written verse.

Such moments, I believe, have created some of my best work.

'Save Me' is about no particular individual, but a series of metaphors about those in my life who are important to me.

You're a lot like lightning
When you light me up
You're like a diamond shining bright
When I'm digging in the rough

You're a lot like time—I can't get enough
You're like a sonnet in a sea of words
When they're all about love

Don't you tell me you are nothing
When you're truly something special to me
Don't you tell me you are nothing
When you're truly something else to me

Without you I'd be lost
Without you I'd be all at sea
You are like a lifeline to me

You're a lot like hope
Something we all need
You're like a welcome spot of sunshine
When I feel the autumn breeze
You're a lot like life
Grown from a seed
You're like a final spot of hope
When I'm begging on my knees

Don't you tell me you are nothing
When you're truly something special to me
Don't you tell me you are nothing
When you're truly something else to me

Without you I'd be lost
Without you I'd be all at sea
You are like a lifeline to me

You're a lot like blood
Running through my veins
You're like a steady heartbeat
When the rest of me's insane
You're a lot like new
When everything's the same
You're like a new forgiveness
When there's only me to blame

Don't you tell me you are nothing
When you're truly something special to me
Don't you tell me you are nothing
When you're truly something else to me

Without you I'd be lost
Without you I'd be all at sea
You are like a lifeline to me

I just need you to save me
You're the one that I need
I finally see
Yes, I finally see
You saved me

Fool on the Run

When we are young, we can often be foolish. We can be blind to risk, and often go through life with blinkers on.

We may glide through the early part of adulthood in a state of delusion, thinking little of consequence.

'Fool on the Run' is a song of reflection about those early years of independence and how we can slowly learn how to navigate life.

When you were young, you laid down your roots
You sold your soul to the sun
So, pack your bags, hide away like the truth
Your mind is shot like a gun
You are just another fool on the run

The days are gone; they fade away
And you've learnt to search for your soul

It doesn't matter if you're young or old
You're still on the lonely road
You are just another fool on the run

What are you running from—can you say?
If it's the truth, it's been and gone far away
Don't ever say I wasn't there for you, come what may
You and I, we're just fools for another day

You made a pact with the devil, son
Now you know there's no looking back
You signed your soul on the dotted line
When your light heart turned to black
You are just another fool on the run

We're all just fools on the run

The Last Chance Saloon

◆》》 ·· ◆ ◆ ·· 《《◆

The classic British pub is getting close to becoming part of the history books.

Pubs are closing at a phenomenal rate, with over five-hundred closing within the United Kingdom in 2023 alone—more than one a day.

When you find a genuine pub, as opposed to the mainstream venues such as the Wetherspoons empire, they can be an inspirational environment for artists.

One such pub I have frequented—The Stanford Arms, in Lowestoft, Suffolk—inspired my song-writing partner, Sean, and I, to write 'The Last Chance Saloon'. The pub's landlord, Lee Baker, is a supporter of original artists, and provides a platform for performers to place their art in front of the public.

Whilst listening to other local artists performing at the venue's Open Mic Night, we grabbed a pen and paper and started jotting down ideas. Twenty minutes later, the pub's new unofficial anthem was finished.

I was walking by the bank of the river
When suddenly, it came to me
That this world is so much bigger
A whole lot bigger than me

I've been in one too many times
Man, all the sights that I've seen
I wish to God that this place
Is the last place I'll ever be

I'm in the Last Chance Saloon
Where the drinks are always free
I'm in the Last Chance Saloon
And there's a price that you'll never see

Oh, I know there's got to be better days ahead
With a future as bright as the moon
But I can't seem to move as I take another drink
In the Last Chance Saloon

I'm in the Last Chance Saloon
Where the drinks are always free
I'm in the Last Chance Saloon
And there's a price that you'll never see

It may seem like I'm stuck in my ways

I can't see the wood from the trees
I feel like I'm on borrowed days
Yet, it's the best that I've ever been

I'm in the Last Chance Saloon
Where the drinks are always free
I'm in the Last Chance Saloon
And there's a price that you'll never see
Yes, there's a price that you'll never see

What Were You Expecting?

We all say and do things we regret, and hindsight is a wonderful thing, once regrettable events have taken place.

If we all took a moment to stop, think, and consider the repercussions of our actions, then I can only imagine that the world would be a much better place.

What were you expecting
When you told me you had left?
You never gave me time to have my say
When you walked out the door
And you threw me to the floor
Then you told me we were going our separate ways

You don't believe in magic
But I believe in miracles today
Because I've seen the second coming

The fire has finally gone away

What was I expecting
When I brought her to resurrection?
Then I removed the seal from our old wounds
When I gave her no options
So, I filled her with corruption
Then I pushed her to the brink way too soon

You don't believe in magic
But I believe in miracles today
Because I've seen the second coming
The fire has finally gone away

The temperature's rising when we're connecting
And we're fighting the lies, like a fine dissection
But we never expected this

What were we expecting
When there was no communication?
Yet there's plenty to say just to get our way
So, we lost all our direction, along with satisfaction
Then we strayed the path
That we once walked in our own way

You don't believe in magic
But I believe in miracles today
Because I've seen the second coming
The fire has finally gone away

We never expected that
We never expected this
We never expected everything to change
Because of a single kiss

Exit Door

There are so many tough decisions to make throughout life.

Sometimes, we just need to face up to reality and accept that things just aren't working out in the way we hoped they would. Walking away is, at times, the best course of action.

I don't see no exit door
I never want to see you around here anymore
But I always know that you're here for me
Yet, I have nothing to offer your family
No, I've got nothing to offer if you have a hold on me

All alone sitting in the shade
Thinking what we could have made
But that's got to go—why can't you see?

I don't want you to have all your hold on me
No, I don't want you to be running around my dreams

But I can't see it all working out for me, no way
Because I'm living a dream—I can't seem to stay
It's one step forward and two steps back again
Going round in circles drives me insane
But at the end of the day, who is truly the one to blame?

So, you're gone and I'm feeling fine
Since you stepped on this heart of mine
But you'll always know just what you've lost
There'll always be that simple line you crossed
I'll never make that line again get lost, no way

I Feel Alive

I have often asked myself, *What is the meaning of life?* When you become a parent, that question suddenly seems easier to answer.

My daughter, Amelie, makes me feel happy, proud, joyful, confident, excited, and, overall, *alive*.

She is my key inspiration for much more than lyrics.

There is nothing I want more in life than for her to grow up being proud to call me her dad.

In *My Verses*, I wanted to ensure that Amelie was the internal bookends, from the dedication through to the last poem. She deserves that honour once more.

She's got all the beauty
That I just can't deny
When she sleeps beside me, I feel alive

She's got all the warmth
That I see in her eyes
When she looks right at me, I feel alive

Oh, this feeling deep inside
Will hold my heart together
And keep me from dying

She's got the sweetest words
That sends my heart into a dive
When she whispers to me, I feel alive

She's got the sweetest touch
She doesn't even have to try
When she holds me tight, I feel alive

Oh, this feeling deep inside
Will hold my heart together
And keep me from dying

She's got all the heart
She's love personified
Forever, she will keep my soul alive

Final Thoughts

I dedicate this book to all those who have inspired me. Not only those who have provided the inspiration to write, but those who are there each and every day. You know who you are, and I am forever grateful.

It is important to find an outlet for our emotions, no matter what those emotions may live.

It can be tiring to hold your feelings within, and I wholeheartedly believe that releasing the valve and allowing your thoughts and feelings to escape is a healthy way to be.

My outlet has always been to write. The vast majority of my work is autobiographical, and even the works of fiction can be sourced back to my own experiences.

I urge you to find your outlet, whatever that may be, and find solace in what you love.

All the best,
Adrian Young

Thank You

Thank you for taking the time to read *More Verses*.
I hope it has been a pleasure for you to read.

As a special thank you, you can access exclusive content,
discounts, and free gifts by signing up to my mailing list,
which you can do by visiting:
https://www.adrianyoungauthor.com/mailing-list

You can also find me via social media platforms:
Twitter: @A_Young_Author
Facebook: Adrian Young – Author

Please consider leaving a review for this book on Amazon
and GoodReads.

Thank you.

Printed in Great Britain
by Amazon